PLAYING INTO SILENCE

Dagger Editions
8100 Alderwood Road,
Halfmoon Bay, BC V0N 1Y1
www.daggereditions.com

Text design by Cara Cochrane
Cover design by Vici Johnstone
Cover photo by Ashley Rowe on Unsplash
Edited by Elizabeth Philips
Printed in Canada

Caitlin Press Inc. acknowledges financial support from the Government of Canada and the Canada Council for the Arts, and the Province of British Columbia through the British Columbia Arts Council and the Book Publisher's Tax Credit.

Library and Archives Canada Cataloguing in Publication

Biello, Tina, 1972–, author
    Playing into silence / Tina Biello.

 Poems.
ISBN 978-1-987915-78-5 (softcover)

    I. Title

PS8603.I343P53 2018   C811'.6   C2018-900753-2

playing into silence

poems

Tina Biello

DAGGER EDITIONS

To my Patty Darling

CONTENTS

PART ONE: CHILDHOOD

What No One Told Me

My breasts were never right. Brown. Small.
Whatever it was, my sister did it first.
When dark hair began to grow between
my legs, no celebration.

"Sally came," was how I learned about blood.
My sister would write that on the calendar
and I knew to stay quiet and retreat
to the forest; I learned to slither.
Leave my questions on some quiet stump while
I foraged for answers.

Once I saw my sister with a bird.
She learned to talk crow,
to caw when danger arrived.
No one told me, this is how you do it.
Love a man this way.

And how to say a woman found me sleeping
in my bed. New Year's Eve she
stole my heart, and fed it to the ravens.
Left me with a Chief Dan George book and her clown nose.
No one told me to love
this way. I told Mom years later,
when her brain had shrunk.
Kathleen, I cawed my lover's
name
into my mother's ear.
She just smiled and walked away.

Knife

1.

Beware the dull Henckel, for it will cut you worse than when it is sharp. It is in disguise as a tool that will help, when it will surely only hinder.

2.

Which came first, the knife or the fork? Which utensil was more useful, the one that would cut the meat or the one that would lift it to a mouth? The modern-day knife is a distant relation to the chopstick, which in Asian culture, can become a weapon, always on hand to use when eating, in case of attack.

3.

Predictably, in any meal, the knife sides with the spoon; in some folk-lore situations, it ran away with the spoon. It is not the loner, rather it protects the lowly spoon, which could not stick up for itself and is better at tricks, like hanging off a child's nose.

4.

Forks may make the difference in roads and rivers, but it's the knife undoubtedly that divides. Says this is this and that is that. The knife may not tune an orchestra like the fork, but it provides the perfect cut of hair from a horse's mane, for the cello bow, that resonant, that clear.

Grade 9 Band

Well I'm so excited. I just got my new saxophone from the bus depot —
it came all the way from Missoula, Montana! My sister found it, a Selmer
Marks VI. Made in Paris.

Finally Mom and Dad are taking me seriously enough that they helped
my buy my first real saxophone. My old one was really falling apart.

The band teacher, Mr. Berkowski, convinced them that someone with
my talent needed a better horn, one that didn't lose its pads or pop
its springs every time you play the keys. So now I'm even getting real
lessons with someone who knows a lot more than my band teacher.
She plays lead alto in the PPCLI military band, the only woman in
the band. She agreed to take me on: Pat Anderson! I think Pat must
be short for Patricia. Mom made me wear this ugly dress. I'm not sure
how she thinks I'll play saxophone in a dress but I wore skorts under-
neath [she lifts her dress].

You see, much better. I think I'll go into the girls washroom and take
off my dress before my lesson, put the dress back on before I go home
and she'll never know.

Heisler Hall Talent Night

She can still hear Ruby Keen and The Bluejays.
The old orchestra play the country dance on a Saturday night.

Her sister has figured out what stair out of ten
creaks at the farm. She carries her down the loft
to the kitchen door, and then they run
the mile into town to the hall.
They watch and air play along
just out of sight, under the porch.
Beer bottles flying
overhead as fights break out.

Tomorrow they will come back
in the sober day
to collect the bottles that didn't break.
Five cents a bottle — they
hum as they work.
Connie, the trumpet parts
and Pam, the saxophone.

Going to the Library, 1963

Today I am going to the library with my book bag, the one Grandpa Clapstein made me. Somewhere in this town it has to exist, a book I'm looking for about this island where women live. It's somewhere far away in a tropical place and very warm. I've heard only women live there and I want to go, leave this shit town Heisler for an Island far away. Last time I asked for a book about women, they gave me *Little Women* to read. I loved it even though there wasn't anything in there about women on an island far away.

I'd rather help my dad than my mom around the house. I like to sit on the roof of his car while he works on it. I have learned how a crankshaft operates, what happens when the rotors are worn down and how the manifold should look under the hood.

But today I am wearing my Sunday finest, even though it isn't Sunday, and I've never been to church. My glasses look smart, even though I'm called 'coke bottle' at school or on some of the bad days, 'Leo the Lion'. I think it might be the duct tape on the arm.

Today I look smart and fourteen years old, grown up. It's Tuesday and Laura always works on Tuesdays. She's the nicest one in the bunch, always helpful and friendly and of course kind of cute. I hope she's there working alone and that the library isn't too busy. Mom will want me home early to help with dinner, but I will pretend I didn't hear her say that. She's so nosy and will ask what I was doing at the library so long. I will lie and say I was reading, when really I'll probably be talking to Laura.

Here's hoping she's alone.

The Harrows

The flax, blue.
The harrows' teeth
were no match for a 12-year-old up from the coulees.
She broke her arm in 2 places, head injured.
It's a wonder she didn't die.

Who could see her playing in the field?
She was warned, stay back.
But this day, the field so inviting, the sky a dome,
she plays dead in the dandelions
so her uncle won't see.
Regrets she didn't bring her sister,
who is left alone with him, drunk.

Who could hear the harrows?
Not Henrietta, not today.
From the gulch to the farmland, an open sky
her breath rising and falling
tiny nipples just swelling
safe in that field of blue.

Heisler

It arrived in Winter, the seed catalogue, on a
January day. It came into town on the afternoon train.

— Robert Kroetsch

Surrounded by coal mines and farms,
Heisler in the1950s, no different from the '20s.
A few more wooden sidewalks, and the hotel newly built.

The old one burned down June 21, 1919. Summer Solstice.
How light lingers in a Prairie sky.

Black smoke made it winter.
Farmers and coal miners came to help,
buckets of useless water from their wells.
The blaze took a few ladies,
men at the bar got out, one leapt on his horse and took off.
Another ran, afraid his wife would smell the booze on him.

1954, the seed catalogue still arrives by train.
A girl with glasses pulls her dog, Skippy, in a sleigh.
She glides down the wooden walkway covered in snow.

Childhood

Remember the windmill well. We used to keep
the cream can down there to keep it cool. We climbed
the ladder down, and looked for salamanders.

Sometimes we got lucky, when no one
was around we'd fling them toward
the house, our protest for having to haul water.
Me, the five gallon pails as my sister followed along.

In winter, we'd get to go to the outdoor skating rink
the Catholic priest made in his backyard.
We all played there, even us Protestants.
'Your dad is crazy', Phil would shout. I warned him,
don't come too near but he did and so I beat him
over the head with a hockey stick, ran home on my skates.
No one called Dad crazy.

Phil's mom started to hang out there, she could tip
a Pilsner back like the rest of them boys.
But my sister and me, we didn't go back.

The West, a Nest and You Dear

> The gopher on his hind legs
> is taut with holiness and fright.
>
> — Lorna Crozier

With you Albertans everything comes down to direction.
East, West, you know the rest —
you can tell where the weather is coming from,
a southeasterly from a northwesterly.
It's written in your DNA.

Highway cop, mighty and stern, smells rain,
the slightest movement of wind against cheek.
He keeps his eyes trained on the road, can tell you exactly
what time the '55 Rambler roared by,
in reverse, toward the farm
that runs the John Deere outlet,
two miles out of town.

Oh yes he knows, record keeper of 56th Ave.
Tonight for Pam's mom he keeps
watch for that Rambler. Records the time,
calls Mrs. Cooper.

1965

1.

Pamela at sixteen, drives a '55 Rambler in reverse
at dusk. The odometer rolls backward, doesn't track
the two extra miles to
Lana's house. Wheels spit
gravel — she's on her way to kiss
her girlfriend goodnight.
Her parents drive up, catch
the kiss, send her
to the asylum.

2.

She plays her saxophone to pass the time.
Indigo notes rise out of the bell, wrap their silky
song around the ears
of the women who sit drugged. A blue-eyed girl
in a wheelchair, in a corner suddenly
stands, waves her arms around like she wants
a partner to fill them, dance her
around the common room.

Pamela keeps on playing, plays to save herself
from sinking
into the same abyss she knew on the farm, when
it was her turn to sleep with
Charlie, the fat Polish farmer who shared the bed
with her Mom, her sister and every other night, with her.

When the charge nurse takes her saxophone away,
she keeps on playing
into the silence, where the notes
are hers and hers alone.

Dust

Two-hundred-year-old burr oak trees
interrupt the view of the tractor.
Wind, and beyond
the trees, dust.

The old Heintzman, silent, for now,
in the middle of her log home.

Crops from last year, dead.
Corn stalks stand like soldiers cut off at the knees.
The news isn't good: another dry year,
crops planted and no water to germinate the seed.

Soy beans are sprinkled across ground,
create a path through Stanley's field.
Poor old Stan, bulldozed his trees last year
and now the wind has taken his soil,
piled it in soft drifts in the ditch.
He waits for the weather to change.

Pot Bellied Stove

The last ember barely red in her
grandmother's kitchen, the one warm heart
in the middle of a Prairie winter.
Grandma Mills half asleep,
boots up on the ledge of the stove,
soles melted from the night before.

King George money safe in sealers
in the root cellar. The mine
long shut down, hole covered up
so cows wouldn't fall in
when they come to graze.

After Dinner Dance

His wife, asleep on the bed.
The cat, a perfect ball.
She breathes, still, silent.
Will she wake?

He hums her a tune, 'Drifting and Dreaming',
years dancing 'round the kitchen table.
Their two daughters, after dinner,
play the tunes they love to dance to.

Take turns. Pam on piano, Connie on trumpet.
Pick a song, trade spots, Pam wants to be done
so she can go play outside, Connie wants to play more
to avoid homework. Connie now plays piano,
Pam, the saxophone.

They play on, argue the whole time. Speed up,
slow down, throw the rhythm off.
Their parents keep dancing:
waltz, foxtrot, rumba,
the old torch songs.

The girls do not notice
Henrietta and Lance, their parents skin to skin
through each song, dancing
their way out
of the coulee shack
into the dance halls,
where they steal the show every time.

Coming home from school she notices Dr. Bellamy's car in the driveway, 1967

All she can think about is last night and Lana's breath on her neck.

Underneath the kitchen window she hears the doctor
talking to her parents:
— How long has this been going on? he asks.
— I found them together last night. I saw them through the cabin
window, her mom replies.
— Were they naked?
— Yes, Doctor, they were.
— Sign here, Mrs. Cooper. I'll take her when she gets home
from school.

Her Dad says nothing.

Party Line

Slim Jim, they call him, he knows
everyone's voice on the party line, everyone knows he
is a rubbernecker, listening in, but that doesn't stop them from talking.
He often embellishes:

Guess what Stanley has done, the old bugger
sent his daughter Gladys to visit an aunt.
We all know what that means.

She was cornered in the tool shed while bringing
slop pails out to the pig trough.

Irwin Kroetsch the postmaster was talking
to Stan about the next train out of town
and how to get her on it.

And that's not all he heard, Slim Jim. He knows
every tale of this town, every
last detail from who's sleeping with whom, what kid
got a spanking for boozing up, to what groceries
were coming in on the train —
rubbernecking Slim Jim, gossip queen of Heisler.

Ponoka

You remember Lana, right?
You remember that we got caught, in the pantry.
Well what I didn't tell you is what happened next:

Pam is in the common room with her saxophone. A girl sits in a wheelchair, staring. Pam sits at a table, puts her saxophone down gently, and gets a deck of cards out of her sax pack. She begins to set up for solitaire. Notices the girl in the wheelchair doesn't talk.

Gee it's really hot in here, don't you think.
It's really hot in here, Pam says louder.
Do you like music?

Keep it down or you'll be removed, the nurse says.

Sorry. They're no fun.

The girl wheels herself over to Pam, touches her hair and then her saxophone

Oh, you do want me to play.
My name is Pam.
What's yours?

That's Sheila. I wouldn't talk to her
or you might find yourself with a black eye.

Nurse moves Sheila away from Pam.

It's ok, nurse, we were just talking.

I'll decide what's ok, dear. You just mind your own business
and keep your game of cards to yourself.

The Lazy Boy

If only she looked at me the way she looks
at that young woman.
I may be a man but I know a thing or two
about women.
She came as the hired help.
You know, she does odd jobs, things I won't do:
dust, clean the toilets, fold the laundry.

Now she's living in the shack, the one up the waterfall.
No electricity, no running water, just a bed
and a woodstove and the bears.
And she loves it.

Ah — if I thought I could kick her out without risking a divorce, I might try.
My wife has grown too accustomed to her and her baking, her smell.
They walk the dogs for hours. When they get home
they think I'm sleeping in the lazy boy by the fire.

I listen, I am
the dog on the scent of rat. I know and feign sleep.
Maybe it's time to get out of this damn chair.
Maybe I'll go see what's going on down the hall.

In the Basement

These are my Black Cat Cigarettes
stolen from Mom's pack, stored
down here by her racks
of Sally Ann clothes, old ghosts
of Heisler's past —
Henrietta's stash, waiting to be mended, waiting to make her
a few bucks.

Me and my cigarettes glow
in the smell of earth and potatoes.
Sent down, kicked out, no supper. What do I care?
I wouldn't eat
with our uncle Charlie, who isn't
our uncle. Mother
the whore. Father the onlooker
and him, the rich pig farmer who promises
Mom gold at the end of her rainbow.
Charlie. Talks treasures to us like the bike
that never arrived or the new baseball glove
he still hasn't bought for my sister.

I can hear them up there — laughing.
As long as he's here, his words drowned
in rye, with his smell of grease
and old spice, I'd rather be down
the hatch, on this dirt floor
in the dark, smoking
my way outta here.

Daysland Hospital

She is two and it's dark. She has figured out
how to climb out of her crib,
tucked in at the wall, at the back of the hospital room.

She sneaks out of the room
with all the babies stuffed in a ward together.
Blanket in hand, she begins the evening under
the bench in the hall, and tries to sleep. She hears a whistle,
time to put the canary to bed
at the nurses station. Listen to it sing
one last time before sleep,
a mother's lullaby.

The nurses know better,
let her sit with them
while they go over each chart,
one at a time, roll call of the sick
and dying.

This little one, with her soft blanket,
whistles to the canary.
The first sunflower to burst open in the garden,
so yellow among the green.

How to Light a Fire

First, the glass. Is it dirty
from last night's fire? If so,
wet a piece of newspaper, dip it in the ash
and wipe the glass clean.

Next, two pieces of wood. Bigger than kindling
yet smaller than a log.
Place them on the bottom of woodstove, one across the other
so there is air beneath them. Every fire
must breathe.

Tear newspaper into strips. Don't bother to read
the headlines.
They will surely contribute to sorrow.

Once strips are laid, rest smaller kindling on top.
Light a match to the paper. Watch.

Take time to linger
on a cold winter day. Spring, a distant cousin
you may never meet.

The Dugout

They used to lose cows in that quicksand,
somewhere in the Rosalind area,
that desert land.
Not only cows but cars,
shoes, dogs and coal miners
went missing.

Somewhere down below,
dinosaur bones. Or so we imagined.

All that's left of Grandma's fruit cellar:
water, lagoon, swamp.
On the prairies they call it a dugout.

Crabapples, paraffin and hooch
flavour the water now. All the cattle know
and come to drink.
This is the most popular dugout
for miles.

Minnewasta Road

She has spent years scraping by,
living on Kraft Dinner, white bread, potatoes.
Morsels, handed to her by her husband
when she least expected it.
To keep her there. Inside the log walls
of the house they built in the '70s,
their fights
in the country, an interruption in the tree line.

During those fall days, while the pumpkins ripened,
she followed her usual routine, making meals, cleaning house
all the while thinking only of
the shotgun hidden in her trunk,
the one used to scare off any coyotes
coming to look for any dog food left around.
Early that October, she tells the kids
tonight's the night:
when Dad, drunk, falls asleep in his chair
the TV turned up

run
one out the east door,
one out the west door
and Connie, the north

Get in the car.
Down Minnewasta road
gravel all the way
to the correction line, straight out of town.

Ronnie, 1945

They bury him at the cemetery. Just outside
the fence, where those families go
who can't afford a burial.

Lance builds his coffin, lucky
it's infant size. He won't have to
gather too much wood.

Ronnie, born in between
here and there, male and
female, sick
and healthy.

Three weeks in the hospital
cost them their house in Heisler.
They would do anything for their first born.
Lose their house and rent
an abandoned bank, make it home.

65 years later
the town of Melville
moved the fence.
gave him a proper headstone.

Klondike Days, Edmonton, 1970

Thumbtacks in hand, she is dressed
in the latest costume
her mother has made for her.
Pam is home to play
honky tonk piano around
town, make some good
bucks to get her through the rest
of her year at university, back in Halifax.

She is off to the oil man's house for a party.
She arrives to a grand piano so big
it has its own revolving stage. One wall
is a salt water aquarium.
She has never been inside a house this size, with
so many rooms and so many beer bottles on the table.
She is taken up on the stage and Dick says,
'have at 'er.'

She takes out her tacks, puts them
in the piano hammers, slowly.
Begins to play
'Sail Along Silvery Moon.'

PART TWO: HOUSE OF STONE

Petroglyph

Spring bursts this meadow open,
flowers light up green moss.

Two women are on foot,
poised to walk through.

I want to tell the youngest to stop.
Turn around, before it's too late.

It is too late. She is going to enter
the meadow, see the snake

on stone. Her own serpent
will rise, slowly.

She will spend
the next seven years waiting.

First Light

I stack her wood, tend her garden, prune her roses.
I always know when she's made love to him, smell him on her.
Tears stain her blue, mascara running down her face —
she wants another drink. Sends me out to get her some more
at the one liquor store on this island.

Wine-stained glasses, dishes not done,
the marrow bones stink up the kitchen as the dogs fight over them.
When I come back with her wine, she is feeding
the raccoons cat food, no matter
how many times I have told her
this is so wrong.

She's never had sex with a woman.
Tells me she prefers it the hard way, the way
she always knew, lying still.
Tonight is different, lips, cool nipples, slow and sure.
Her skin aches, too much softness for one night.
Before dawn, the snow will bear witness.
Who else will believe this tale?
I am sworn to silence.
She wants it both ways.
Soft hands, rough face.
A story I cannot tell.

Blue Lake

The neon lights read
Half Moo Motel, the N burnt out.

She sleeps beside me.
It is 5 am.
The birds at home
will be waking soon:
junco, chickadee, towhee.

Here in the city, the crows,
black dots in the sky,
will sing the dawn song
to annoy all humans who sleep.

Why can't I love the crow?

Soon my lover will leave.
Kiss me and say, a couple of months isn't that long,
it's my last gig down there.
Pack her tap shoes, clown nose and Diablo
and catch the Greyhound for Blue Lake.

At 5:30, the crows will begin.

Fish Tank

She plays her saxophone to her fish.
A pastime to
fill the hours left to her by her ex lover.
The fish keep watch in her bedroom,
who comes, who goes.

Here on this small island, she has no prospects.
She plays what the fish swim. Draws a staff
on the side of the glass.
They rise and fall with each half note, whole note.

Today the house cleaner, clad
in rags and carrying a bucket, stops
to admire the fish.
What is that on the glass?
Should she clean it?

The fish tank seems out of bounds.
This house, the drums, the sage.
She could crawl right in. Make herself at home.

The fish watch on.
Swim the music on the side of their home.
Somehow she hears the song, knows she will return.

Anonymous Woman

Watch out for those straight women, she was warned
by all her lesbian friends.
You know the kind,
they seep into you, telling you they've never
slept with a woman but love hanging out
with gays. Oh the fag hags.
They drench your skin in sweat when you smell them close
and then they disappear.

Watch out.
Don't be fooled by the pretty hair or eyes
or gorgeous fitting dresses.
Oh what a hottie,
you may think.
That is the beginning of the end.

For hidden in her pants or dress or
business suit, lies a woman
who wants but doesn't, and can't
and you will begin the descent.
Before you know it,
you are trapped in her smell
and her red hair
that will never come to you.

Love Song

She is alone again. In her bed.
Leonard Cohen tunes play in her ear.

Her lover calls. Condensation
drips down the bedroom window.

A streak catches her eye.
Her lover's voice and Leonard's in tune.

She never could sing.
Perhaps that is why she loves

his music. Drunken notes. Drunken voice.
She watches the water bead. Hangs up.

This was supposed to be a love poem.
But the fountain ran out of water.

She ran out of breath and
her lover ran out of booze.

She lights a fire. Warms her feet,
as her lover turns to someone new.

Standing in the Cedar Grove

The ravens, who mated today, are asleep now, hidden
in the cedars. The woman stands directly under the birds, cannot see
her hand in front of her, although she sees into the window
of the house she watches.
The stars
are out.

A woman is lying on the couch.
She is not with her dogs or her cat,
but the husband she said she was leaving
who is sitting with her head in his lap.

The woman outside should not be watching,
She is the other
woman. Frozen
here.

Above her one of the ravens
squawks, begins to wake
as dawn approaches.
The woman will leave, this time,
but not for good.

Nocturne

Inside those eyes a snow leopard
lurks, frost on his whiskers.

At night when you get ready for bed, he waits
at your feet, eyes me

into place. I make room
for his royal presence. He settles
on your chest, rocks you
to sleep.

I reach over
to hold you. Feel the softness of his back, the heat
of his breath. The Himalayas

beckon him,
where his tail navigates
the hunt. When you sleep, I watch
as you join him for these hours.

I hold you now, soft moon belly, nipples
pert from the cold. I know

when morning breaks, you will be back.

On the dirt road between sunset and moon rise

The cows in the field gather; soon
it will be dark.
We are walking down the road
between two farms, heading for the forest,
the dogs, their last duty walk before sunset.

I am silent, as always. She doesn't shut up,
constantly talks —
kids, husband, garden, the play she's directing, how her boots
are falling apart from all the walking and she really must
buy new ones.

The dogs on the end of the leash
pulling pulling pulling.

She finally brings up the weekend, the trip
we have planned,
a drive off Island, to the city, go see a movie.
Bad news, she can't make it, has run out of excuses.

I am silent. I know if I say
something, we'll have another fight.
Who would believe me about the last one, the bruises?
Who would believe that earlier that day we were lovers?
Who would believe me?
I don't even believe myself.

October: Ladybugs

Thousands descend on her log home.
They fly across the dirt road from the burr oak forest,
land on this other forest she calls her home.

The ladybugs don't notice any difference,
in fact Connie's forest is easier on the feet.

The soy bean field had a bad aphid year,
farmers brought in those Asian ladybugs and now

Charka, the white Pyrenees, is decorated red and black,
perfect for the month of Halloween.

He doesn't think it's funny. Goes mad
trying to pick them off his fur,
like he does in wood tick season.

She must go out carrying an umbrella
so they don't land on her face.

Look

Magpie at the cemetery
has found a spot to bury
all things shiny.

Those who don't look down
will not find what they came for.

Better Days

One thing I know: every year
the varied thrush will come to eat

crabapples out of reach,
Winter's bounty.

Blue-eyed gaze. I am caught in a world
of mushy peas, Stilton cheese and Yorkshire pudding.

Vanilla beans rattle in their pods, to become
perfume for her skin. This will corrupt her lover.

Legend has it the spirit of a tree
is trapped inside its stump

if the faller did not turn his back while
taking the tree.

Winter has laid her claim on my garden.
Frogs sing their love song in the mud.

Wait for the heat of better days to come.

One More Time

(An orchestra sits down to rehearse, tune their instruments to the oboe, A440. Two musicians in the cello section wait their turn.)

How old were you when you had your first girlfriend? he asks the older woman.

Where did that question come from?

I don't know. I just want to know. Why haven't I found a boyfriend yet?

First, you need to leave home, dear Allan. You'll never get laid with that mother of yours around.

What?

It's the truth, she says.

I know but how did you do it? You lived at home and got laid. When did you first kiss a girl?

I was sweet 16 and in pursuit. No easy task on the prairies in 1965. But I knew I had to find someone interested in kissing a girl.

Did you always know you were a lesbian?

Yes! Especially when I found Lana, the tall blond with the farm and horses just outside of town. She was the only girl I could convince to kiss another girl. She had the perfect property. We would go horseback riding way out where her mom couldn't catch sight of us, dismount and tie up our horses. Find a patch of grass and start rolling.

I had to be careful. I knew my mom would be onto me. Lana's mom let us sleep together in their cabin and would only check in on us before bedtime. I always wished I had a mom like that.

My God Allan I think it's time you left home. How old are you?

(The conductor taps his baton on the music stand, gets their attention.)

Night, Time

The bed is filled with water.
It is never still. Now that she has broken
her leg she is stuck
on a mattress that makes her sea sick. Throughout the day
a revolving door of dogs, kids, grandkids.
Empty wine glasses from last night
on the headboard. Her lover comes and goes,
bringing her food, and tea in bone china.
All day she writes on pieces of paper, tucks them
in a journal with her name on it: Carolyn.
The ring from her lover never worn in public
is on today.
A golden circle on the wrong finger.
Now that her husband has come home,
she has taken it off.

At three am
her husband hears the lamp click on.
Who will bring her another cup of tea?

The dog hears a rustling,
mouse in the garden.
Tomorrow the dog will kill.
When the sun rises, when the shadows
are gone.

My Pearls

I would like her to wear them to bed tonight.
I'll tell her it's a favour for me — her mistress.
Please warm them so the pearls won't
give me a chill,

I won't tell her the real reason —
to have her smell on me.

While he dances me around the ballroom
I will be looking into her eyes. His hands, her hands
in disguise.
He will think I am swooning for him,
all the while keeping her so close.
The pearls around my neck.

When she arrives to dress me, I will give her
the pearls, that my scent will mix with hers
one more day and night, this last one
as her mistress.

For after the wedding my thoughts of her will be
gone.
She will weep and in ten years,
after the fights and the children, only then
will I be brave enough to call on her.
To dress me, and then
to undress me
like he never could.

Seduction

Beaverbank, Nova Scotia. Winter. Christmas parties everywhere. The
story has played out in my mind these forty-two years. Why couldn't
I see it coming? Was I too drunk? That's what we did then, drink and
drive home. My friend Joan with the brand new 1972 Mercedes hard
top convertible. She was always a bit crazy, drank to the point of pure
dark. I did want to ride in it, though. That night I said yes. I didn't know
she wanted more, wanted the ride to take us to her house. She never did
like homos; I was sure she wasn't lesbian, but her hands said otherwise.
I asked her to slow down. She turned up the stereo, pretended not to hear.
The last corner was the one. End
                                over end, we hit the ditch. The cabin
intact. I got out of the car, head bleeding. Joan walked away without a
scratch. In the hospital later, she asked me to take the valium out of the
glove box, in the car compound, in case they accused her of intoxication.

I wonder now who was it that Joan wanted to kill?

The Crossing

My ex-lover rides the ferry, back
and forth, back and forth. Some days
it's for an appointment,
other days just for the hell of it.
The fog on this island seeps into her bones,
draws out the blue in her eyes.

She survives by riding — the one road on the island gets tedious —
catches the wind
of the eagle at the dock, watches
kingfisher helicopter, and dive for food.

You're looking great, she says to me,
the day I see her in town
walking to the liquor store.

Her cheeks rosy, that damned rosacea
brightens her up every sip
she takes, the wind adds to
her colour the way blush never could.

Sylvie

Who was your first crush? I ask at my group. Sylvie says, 'oh that's easy, it was a girl'. The room goes quiet. She takes herself to her first high school crush — Marie-Claire, the blond who the nuns adored. So did Sylvie. She wished she could climb right into that strawberry blonde, wrap it around her bosom, kiss her tiny nipples just about to bloom.
Ah, but we are here now. 2:24 pm, Minds in Motion, socializing. A room full of straight, demented, and not so demented couples. Sylvie blushes, but only a little. Her smile, coy as she wraps her scent around Marie-Claire. Jim, the Scotsman, reaches for more tea and a 'bikky'. The room, silent, for one sweet moment while I move on to the next question.

ODS

She talks about aging in humorous acronyms,
ODS: Old Dyke Syndrome.

All the failings of an aging body:
cataracts that cloud her day, hearing
aids that whistle too loud as the battery
dies, and beer that tastes so bad, may as well have club soda.

Her yoni dry, she waits for a lover.

Inside the humour you hear the tears.
A white noise, the kind that keeps you awake
even though it's meant to block out the city racket.

Having known life on the run
she is happy to be still.
Out and in her full glory
of a big butch woman.

In 20 years who will love her and tuck her in?
Will she live in one of those homes back in a closet
as the straight couples kiss in the dining room?

The old demented ones will think she's a man,
ask when her wife will visit.

She will smile and say,
Oh I can't wait — she is coming today at lunch.

To the wine glass she clutched every night

You are free as she quit
three years ago.
Sometime in between the affair, the divorce, the move,
I'm sure you broke.

I raise a glass to you now.
You seduced her, comforted
her and fed our fights.

You lie now shattered
somewhere in the landfill,
threaten the feet of ravens
looking for scraps.

Tai Chi

Step up and raise hands!
I glimpse my reflection in the window.

What comes next? Oh yes,
white stork spreads wings.

Feathers rise out of my neck and shoulders.
Push up against the person behind me.
She doesn't notice. She is busy
brushing her left knee, strumming
the pei pa.

I am fully crane now.
I wrap my wings
around my heart.

Red Snapper

Did you know a red snapper's heart will beat
long after the fish is dead?
So says Isaac. Telling us about his fishing trip,
he motions with his index finger and thumb
how he beats the hearts back to life, while
the fish lie flat. The heart extracted
from their mouths with a hook.

One, two, three, four,
hearts brought to life
beating in front of him on the boat deck.
Timpanis in his orchestra.

He knew this was how it worked.
Too many switches working his
valves. Electrical currents running too fast, tachycardia.
His heart stopped,
started again.

Body flat in ER.
Thirty-one and he didn't say good-bye to his wife.
The red snappers' hearts
all around him, thumping. They

brought him back. The fish,
like fish do, followed the scent home.

Cortona, Summer Heat

In this house of stone, we have told our story.
The one where a woman loves a woman.
In a town where the church bells ring every hour.
We have come to a country that has forgotten women.

And Silvio, the retired race car driver
knocks at the wrong moment, sensing
serpents in his midst. Here
to remind us about tomorrow,
our boat ride at the lake.

Somewhere the tricksters are laughing,
and the matriarchs of my lineage have shown up
to cheer us on.

They ask us to please hold hands in the streets.
Make them look. Make them
wonder. Make them
love again.

PART THREE: A GOOD PLACE

Township Road 424

It's September, 2013, and we have come back to remember. Connie
came with her son years ago and they couldn't find them. When the
bus let us off after school, we found the gate where we went in was
always down. Someone must have removed the gate, or all the roads
look the same to us now.
We have been driving for two hours in squares, the grid roads haven't
changed. Each farmer we stop to ask about how to find the coulees,
says he has never heard of the coulees or the mine shafts around here.
Sorry ladies, can't help you.
Connie remembers that Grandma Mills' shack in the coulees was off
the Correction Line Road. By now our water bottles have warmed up
and the snacks are long eaten. It's hot for September and we have been
driving way too long. These farm roads outside of Heisler would warm
anyone's blood.
We started the day in stories:

Remember Pete Lasoo, the egg grader on Main street,
drunk. Sitting in the dark, with a single bulb,
shooing us away,
as we watched him grade eggs.
He would try to get rid of us, give us quarters and we would buy licorice,
jawbreakers, satchel popcorn and
come right back to watch him work.

At the end of the day we are still looking for the leached coulee,
driving Township 424.
The stories have come and gone and now the heat is thick.
The gate, it should be down, it always was.
Just before we give up, we find it.
Twenty years later, they fixed that gate, cows getting out too often.
We look at each other,
this is it.

Jawbreakers sucked down to the licorice seed.

A Prairie Gathering

Sit around with a cup of instant coffee,
toothpick in hand, then to mouth.
Talk as though it isn't there.

We discuss coyotes, mosquitoes,
grouse, cattle and shotguns.
Will the saskatoons produce this year?
How many times did Mom and Dad come to visit?
What did the neighbour do with his dugout?

In Connie's kitchen the chrome legs shine.
Yellow Arborite. Her swivel chairs
her brown swivel chairs,
still swivel.

To the green chair he sat in every night to watch *Jeopardy*

You held him steady,
even though you rocked a little
while he nodded off
as the wine kicked in.

You took his weight.
Less every year.
as his appetite faded.

Only you could touch him. Sometimes
the phone rested on your arm
as he waited for me to call —
I didn't.

Alone, you consoled him.
After Mom died, he folded
her knit blanket, placed it neatly
on your back, every night.

Connie's Place

Noon day sun in May, warm enough to sit out for awhile.
Birds decorate the feeders.

The odd car races down the dirt road,
creates a storm in its wake.

In a world of remote access, Wi-Fi, cell phone buzz
nothing works here. We are off the grid.

Oriole
white breasted nuthatch
red winged blackbird
finch
chickadee
on the porch wind chimes tuned to Big Ben
call this breeze home.

1967 Massey-Ferguson
sits with weighted discs and an oil can rusted,
upside down over the exhaust
stops the rain from getting in,
if we do get any rain, that is.

Machine Rot

In this heat, dust and spear grass,
an old Massey-Ferguson hunkers in the field.

Who drives those anymore?
Discs their rows, weeds out the grass and ticks,
so the saskatoons don't choke,
live one more year.
They are 28-year-old bushes, usually only live 25.
Who drives an old Ferguson?

Connie does. Her machines do not rot
on the margins of her property.
They are well oiled, well used.
Toothpick between her teeth,
410 shotgun leans in the stairwell
to scare away any coyotes coming to look for trouble.

Maggots

1.

To eat what's dead
in order to live.
Remember this at every meal,
the maggot does.

2.

An adult female fly lives one month.
During this time she lays 2000 eggs, in batches.
Her belly always filled with babies,
soon to be maggots.

3.

A prisoner was dying of gangrene
in a concentration camp during the war, his foot black.
The German officer placed maggots on his toe and ankle.
They ate his dead skin, kept him alive.

4.

Why are so many women afraid of snake, worm, maggot?
The slither should be familiar.

5.

She cuts his toenails before work, his feet well manicured.
The clippings hit the ground.
He doesn't tell her about the chicken,
forgotten in the garbage bag
in the corner of the garage,
moving.

6.

A fly in summer, the maggots are never far behind.

Coal

This was a time of innocence,
folks in coulee shacks down by the mines. Each tipple
a steeple, a landmark. Dollar signs
in the sky for these hooch-loving hillbillies.

Cold mornings, the pot bellied stove burns
the last of its embers. No one
awake enough to stoke it.

Mantle lamp out,
dead moths around the base, sacrificed themselves
for one touch.

Now all that's left:
rusted cars, missing parts
scattered. The door to the stove
in the cattle field. Dinosaur bones
safely underground.

Rainbow Bridge

My sister dreams about our dead uncle.
He tells her our mother, also dead, is beyond him.
A place higher than he can go. The rainbow bridge,

the nine-rung ladder will lead you there,
in Tibet. You will be greeted by the great
winged Garuda. His eagle nose will sniff out
your sincerity. Don't be afraid,
it is a good place.

Angels are not
cherub-faced chubby children.
No, the angels she saw:
teardrop strands of light
on her lungs, lighting there and shooting off.
She in a coma, unable to tell anyone

the good news.
The trees know best.
Stay rooted in the underworld —
but reach for the heavens.

Stan Reynolds Museum, Wetaskiwin, Alberta

— You know they don't make alternators like they used to.
— No they sure don't.
— You know I'm sure Dad welded a lot of these steam engines.
— Yup, I'm sure he did.

Walking through the museum, they can hear their
ancestors fight in the hum of
the lights behind the old gas pump.
One of the girls spots the red pedal car, high up on a beam,
out of reach, just like when they were kids in Heisler.

Stopping by the washrooms by the old
T-Bird, they catch sight of a video playing:
how to fix rust embedded in frames, make
them new again.

Both gals stop and watch. Completely taken in,
forgetting they have to pee.

— Do you think my mechanic would do this to my old GMC Sierra?
— Maybe.
— Dad would have for sure if he were still alive.
— Yup.

Lance smiles from his perch, wherever he is now. He taught
his daughters well.
An echo in the hills beyond the coulees. Sunrise.
His daughters: the sons he never had.

Acknowledgments

I have deep gratitude to Patrick Lane and Lorna Crozier, and the many retreats over the years where many of these poems were born. This book is edited by Elizabeth Philips, a gifted editor who has brought my work to a whole new level. Thank you. And finally, thank you to both my family and my LGBTQ family who lived through some tough times. You are all amazing and inspiring.

Notes

p. 12: "Knife" is after Lorna Crozier's poem "Fork" from *The Book of Marvels: A Compendium of Everyday Things* (Greystone Books, 2012).

p. 17: Epigraph for "Heisler" is from Robert Kroetsch's *Seed Catalogue* (Turnstone Books, 1977).

p.19: Epigraph for "The West, a Nest and You Dear" is from Lorna Crozier's "A Prophet in his own Country" from *The Blue Hour of the Day: Selected Poems* (McLelland & Stewart, 2007).

p. 51: "My Pearls" is after Carol Ann Duffy's poem "Warming Her Pearls" from *Selling Manhattan* (Anvil Press Poetry, 1987).